TO: _____

FROM: _____

Praise for Ted Larkins's
GET TO BE HAPPY

"I really loved this book. *Get To Be Happy* is accessible, digestible, and practical. It's a powerful reframe for anyone struggling to come to a new perspective."
—John "Roman" Romaniello, *New York Times* bestselling author

"Ted Larkins has written a fantastic chronicle of his amazing life experiences. *Get To Be Happy* is funny, honest, joyous, sad, candid, engaging, moving, and emotional. More importantly, it is inspirational. Ted shares his philosophy of finding the positive side of any situation and challenges the reader to achieve a more healthy, balanced, and tranquil lifestyle."
—Charles Riotto, president, Licensing Industry Merchandise Association (LIMA)

"This book is amazing! It keeps in the spirit of life between the birth and death of every human being. It is an incredible experience and reminds us of the important things that happen to all of us—I am deeply impressed and love it."
—Joachim Knödler, managing director, CPLG Germany/France

THE
GET TO
PRINCIPLE

A SIMPLE TECHNIQUE TO CREATE INSTANT JOY

How to Get Happy, Get Going, and Get To It in Life

TED LARKINS

Copyright © 2020 by Ted Larkins
Cover and internal design © 2020 by Sourcebooks
Cover design by Lindsey Cleworth

Sourcebooks, the colophon, and Simple Truths are registered trademarks
of Sourcebooks.

All rights reserved. No part of this book may be reproduced in any form or by any
electronic or mechanical means including information storage and retrieval systems—
except in the case of brief quotations embodied in critical articles or reviews—without
permission in writing from its publisher, Sourcebooks.

This publication is designed to provide accurate and authoritative information in regard
to the subject matter covered. It is sold with the understanding that the publisher is not
engaged in rendering legal, accounting, or other professional service. If legal advice
or other expert assistance is required, the services of a competent professional person
should be sought.—*From a Declaration of Principles Jointly Adopted by a Committee of
the American Bar Association and a Committee of Publishers and Associations*

All brand names and product names used in this book are trademarks, registered
trademarks, or trade names of their respective holders. Sourcebooks is not associated
with any product or vendor in this book.

Photo Credits
Internal images © pages viii, 80, Hero Images/Getty Images; page xii, Klaus Vedfelt/
Getty Images; page 4, Maskot/Getty Images; pages 10, 22, 92, 108, Westend61/Getty
Images; page 34, Halfpoint Images/Getty Images; page 72, PeopleImages/Getty Images;
page 74, Caiaimage/Paul Bradbury/Getty Images; page 76, Luis Alvarez/Getty Images;
page 96, MoMo Productions/Getty Images; page 110, Oliver Rossi/Getty Images; page
112, Ippei Naoi/Getty Images
Internal images on pages xv, xvi, xx, 16, 26, 32, 38, 40, 42, 44, 48, 52, 54, 56, 58, 62, 64,
68, 86, 90, 94, 98, 104, 115, and 116 have been provided by Unsplash; these images are
licensed under CC0 Creative Commons and have been released by the author for public use.

Published by Simple Truths, an imprint of Sourcebooks
P.O. Box 4410, Naperville, Illinois 60567-4410
(630) 961-3900
sourcebooks.com

Manufactured in Singapore.
OGP 10 9 8 7 6 5 4 3 2 1

FOR
NIA & WILL

CONTENTS

INTRODUCTION

"YOU'RE BORN AND THEN YOU DIE, AND IN BETWEEN, YOU GET TO DO THIS THING CALLED LIFE!"

I'm excited. I **get to** write this book. Through writing, I **get to** share not only ideas that have percolated in my mind for years but also ideas that have yet to emerge from this unfolding, yet-to-be-experienced life. I **get** to be who I have become and become even more through writing. I also get to be part of who you are becoming as you read this. These words are part of the evolving you, and you get to accept, reject, and ponder the concepts and images these words convey. Every moment is like that. Every breath, every sip of water, every interaction, every moment, good or bad, becoming who you are. You get to take part in the universal urge to create and become something better than you are now by becoming the best you can be. Oh yeah, we get to, all right!

OK, OK, I went a little overboard with the Get Tos in that opening paragraph. I promise that's not what this book is all about. Yes, you're going to Get To throughout these pages. But this isn't your average self-help book that scratches the surface of the human experience and creates a temporary respite from the challenges of life with some cute, catchy phrase. The Get To Principle is a jumping-off point into a mindset, a way of being that supports you in creating who you are destined to be in your life. It *can* be magical. And I don't mean magical as in creating things out of thin air, but rather as in building up who you are so that things you want come into your life—*almost* magically.

The Get To Principle, when embraced, will lead to a deeper knowing of yourself, a look inward that creates what you have on the outside and creates lasting change. The early-twentieth-century writer James Allen wrote, "It matters everything what you are within, for everything without will be mirrored and colored accordingly."

Although many of the concepts around Get To are simple, they can have a positive effect on all areas of your life. As an executive coach and corporate trainer, I assist all levels of management in applying Get To in order to look into who they are so that real change can happen in the workplace. You'll see in part 3 how you can apply some of the Get To practices in your company. I use Get To with my family, which allows for deeper and happier communication between us. Yes,

even with my teenagers! And of course, personally, it's changed how I live my life as I awaken to what I truly want to experience. By the end of our journey here, I hope you feel the same.

Our lives are filled with commitments, obligations, responsibilities, and to-do lists that read like novels. How about your to-do list? Is it like a telephone book and you're on *A*? For many of us, as soon as we wake up, often with hearts racing in panic for the coming day, it's an insanity of running from one thing to another, sure that each one is as important as the one before. Time is passing, and we complain that we just can't slow it down.

Are you ready for a change? Get To is a way out, a lifeline to getting back to sane. It is a simple but profound, challenging but fun way to live life.

Here's the thing about the Get To Principle: we've forgotten that each moment alive on the planet as a human is a miracle. Our bodies are bundles of energy made up of over fifty trillion cells. Each cell contains over three feet of DNA. This DNA stretched out would wrap around the earth two million times. These human bodies that we call ourselves are wonders of energy and complex systems that work every second of the day from birth to death, keeping us alive. They are the most advanced structures in the known universe and amazing flows of energy that our five (six if you quiet your mind enough) senses turn into this experience we call life.

But in the midst of everyday life, bills to pay, children and aging parents to take care of, relationships to navigate, and bodies to keep healthy, how do we tap into that feeling, the "knowing" that we are so lucky, blessed, or simply fortunate to have these moment-to-moment experiences? How do we access the understanding that our abilities to be aware we're even having these experiences are monumental achievements of consciousness? And most important, how do we create and have meaning and joy in our everyday lives?

Our lives are filled with uncertainties that, if feared, lead to resisting what is happening and missing all the glory of the present moment. People are searching for relief from the burdens of everyday life, looking for the clarity of living more fully but rarely finding it. We feel that we are victims of our lives and often have grief that never seems to go away. Many of us are disgruntled with the confusing and often contradictory messages of our religions and the various new age and spiritual teachings, and we have given up hope. Using the Get To Principle changes all that.

I share what I share so that people can experience aliveness, right in this moment. I share because in doing so, I remember to wake up and truly live. In an obscure but powerful book on understanding human potential, *You Are the Adventure*, J. Allen Boone says that "within each of us is a never-satisfied hunger for greater freedom of being and expression, and with it an almost constant urge to find new ways to get more out of life, ways that will be more productive and satisfying than those offered by the material senses."

Don't get me wrong, I like comforts and luxuries as much as the next person. But when having nice things is not the goal, when sitting quietly listening to the wind in the trees or watching a sunset is more important than what is on the cell phone screen, life takes on a whole new meaning.

How about you? *What do you want in life?*

PART
ONE

HOW TO CHANGE "I'M AWFUL" INTO "I'M ACTUALLY PRETTY AWESOME"

"THE REWARD FOR CONFORMITY IS THAT EVERYONE LIKES YOU EXCEPT YOURSELF."
—RITA MAE BROWN

ONE

THE KILLER OF THE "HAVE TO" MINDSET

Most people think the first thing we say as babies is *mama* or *dada*. But I think the first thing we say is "I have to." After all, what infants hear most of the day from their parents is "I have to make a bottle. Will you hold them?" "I have to change her," and "I have to calm him."

From there, it's downhill as children hear all that they have to do, and the list just grows as they do: "I have to go to work," "I have to play with the kids,"

"I have to go to the store," "I have to take the kids to school." It is, to many of us, the way it is—you just have to do things.

Our language and our nervous systems work together to create our environment. We often think that we use language to describe the world when, in fact, we use language to create the world and how we experience it. "I have to" is a structure that our society lives by and we follow obediently. What we fail to realize is that saying "I have to" is the underlying source of much of our stress. It's assuming that we have no control in what is happening in our lives.

Say "I have to" out loud right now. "I have to." Can you feel that feeling? When you really feel "I have to," when you look behind the **indoctrinated ease** of saying it, an undefinable feeling of almost dread comes over you. It's a "You better or else…" kind of feeling. Lurking is the question "And if I don't?" We don't answer that. We just keep going, **having to** do our lives. "I have to go get a cup of coffee." Underlying that phrase is a real *bummer*. It can be debilitating. In essence, we have become victims to most of life's circumstances.

Saying "have to" has been part of the English language since, well, Shakespeare: "Then what I **have to** do/Will want true color—tears perchance for blood." Everyone says some version of "I have to," whether it's "I gotta," "I should," "I'd better," or even "Yeah, whatever, I'll do it." But therein lies the problem. We are so enmeshed in it, it's so a part of who we are, that we can't see it. We are it. We live as victims, in dread and fear (after all, if we don't do it, something bad will obviously happen) through that simple "have to" phrase—and we don't even know it.

So how do you change from a lifetime of saying "I have to" and start moving into a more powerful way of being? Start by changing your mindset.

TWO
ENTERING A GET TO MINDSET

We all have moments in our lives when we wake up feeling that there's more to life than the grabbing up of things. One day, I was doing the dishes, grumbling about some recent work stuff. Doing the dishes can be a crappy job in the best of times, but I had recently foreclosed on nine real estate properties and filed for bankruptcy, so it was extra painful this day. But as I scrubbed, a thought came to me, and I remembered that some twenty thousand people die of starvation on the planet each day. I said to myself, "I just had a great meal. Wow, I got to have a great meal." As I continued to scrub, I thought, "Even with all that suffering, at least I get to do the dishes." I smiled. Doing the dishes suddenly wasn't that bad.

As I finished the dishes and was heading to my computer to face my dreaded, bank-notice-filled inbox, my wife reminded me I had agreed to play with my eleven-year old son, Will. I sighed and mumbled, "Oh, I have to play with Will." As I walked toward him, playing on the floor with a sophisticated LEGO of some sort, I remembered a recent school shooting and how many parents wouldn't have an opportunity to play with their kids tonight. I thought to myself, "Dude, you **get to** play with your boy. What did we **just** do with the dishes?" Although I had had many "get to" moments throughout life, it solidified in the next step I took. I realized that saying "I get to" is a powerful frame of mind to be in. I also realized that if I said it deliberately, I could maintain the powerful mindset at will. I sat down on the floor with Will in a sense of awe.

To be clear, I'm not saying you don't "have to" do things. After all, if you don't do the dishes, they'll pile up and stink. If you don't go to work, you won't get money to pay the bills, and it will suck. However, step beyond that victim mentality of *have to*, making the shift instead to *get to*, and your life immediately changes for the positive.

As you start using the Get To Principle, a simple concept starts to well up in your mind: It's really not all that serious. As you start saying "I get to," your mind gets quiet, you smile more, and doing the tasks at hand seems easier. As Daniel Kahneman says, "*Nothing is as important as you think it is, at least when you are thinking about it.*"

There are three steps I recommend when building a mindset around the Get To Principle:

1 *Say* "get to" when you otherwise "have to."

2 *Smile* and take a beat.

3 *Do it*.

First, when you **say** "get to," your mind automatically becomes quiet, if only for a moment. When I surveyed people practicing the Get To Principle, I learned that they believe that saying "get to" brings a sense of peace of mind. Simply saying "I get to" in any situation created a feeling of **compassion and gratitude**, which had a calming effect overall.

With **compassion and gratitude**, there is sincere understanding of the suffering of others. Compassion is an inherent human quality. There's a difference between feeling sorry for someone and having compassion. Feeling sorry for someone is filled with guilt, because you have what you have and the other person doesn't. Feeling sorry is about yourself. Compassion is filled with love and caring and simply being present with the other person, available to help where possible. This is an immediate response to saying "I get to." Try it now. Sit quietly and say "I get to." Can you feel that?

Now, in that calm space of mind, *smile*. Smiling releases positive endorphins in your body, and you feel joy. In a *Huffington Post* blog post called "The Science of Smiling," Andrew Merle said, "It seems that the simple act of a physical smile, authentic or not, tricks your brain into thinking you're actually happy. Smiling also triggers us to think back to joyful memories, further improving mood." Fake it till you make it? Why not? Other research has shown that smiling people are friendlier overall and that the joy transfers to other people. As Rocky might have said, "Smile, Adrian. It's all we got."

Next, from that space of compassion, appreciation, and now joy, *do what you were going to do*. This "do it" step is the key to a successful life. We've all made resolutions, most of us have goals, and we've promised

ourselves or others that we're going to change, but we often don't. In reality, true change comes only when the current reality is acknowledged, the desired result is stated, and **action toward that desired result** is practiced. The change can happen in an instant or over time. In the Get To state of mind, action becomes easy and change happens. We'll look at this more fully in chapter 6.

I will often repeat these steps to myself, making them into a mantra of sorts. The "Get To, Smile, Do It" mantra can be voiced prior to doing something, or as I've found more often, while you're doing it. For example, one night at 11:00 p.m. with work still to do for the morning, I begrudgingly got into the car to go pick up medicine at the twenty-four-hour drugstore for my daughter, Nia, who was feeling sick. As I started the car, I said, "Get To, smile, go get medicine." In that moment, the grudge lifted, and I felt blessed beyond words that I had a car and wasn't walking in the snow to the store, and that we lived so close to a drugstore that

Nia was able to so quickly get medicine. Heck, I felt grateful I didn't live in another era where I was heading out to a tribal elder to get slugs to put on her face. My life was truly blessed. And as it turns out, my life seems to be blessed more often than not.

The other day, I showed up at a restaurant to meet a friend for lunch, but at the last minute she texted saying she couldn't make it. My initial WTF in a second turned into "Get To, smile, read a book I have in my car while I have a good meal." What a blessing! In *Outwitting the Devil*, a book Napoleon Hill wrote a year after releasing his renowned *Think and Grow Rich* in 1937, he wrote, "I have also discovered that there comes with every experience of temporary defeat, and every failure and every form of adversity, the seed of an equivalent benefit." In other words, if you look, there are blessings in everything.

I use these steps like a mantra all day, and I am consequently refocused on my blessings instead of my problems. In fact, I am actually reshaping my problems *into* blessings. When I'm resisting a workout, doing the dishes, waking up, getting the kids ready for school, having a discussion with my wife, feeding the cat, and cleaning the litter box—I **get to**. I **smile**. And I **do it**. It's powerful. I am becoming stronger and more of a creator of my life. This has led to an underlying state of contentment. Yes, I still feel crappy sometimes. And I have bad moods. And I resist paying bills. But not as much and not for as long. The habit of Get To is now part of my life, and I experience more joy more often. I experience feeling pretty awesome a lot of the time.

And you can too.

PART TWO

HOW TO BE FREE OF THE MIND

"ALL THAT IS HARMONY FOR YOU, O UNIVERSE, IS IN HARMONY WITH ME AS WELL."
—MARCUS AURELIUS

THREE
THE LENS OF LIFE—SHAPING YOUR REALITY

I've watched dozens of TED Talks. There is great learning to be done watching those incredible people share their ideas and stories. One in particular stands out for me: Shawn Achor's talk, "The Happy Secret to Better Work." In between the great storytelling and laughs, he said something quite poignant: "It's not necessarily the reality that shapes us, but the lens through which your brain views the world that shapes your reality."

What is the lens through which we're viewing our

realities? Our beliefs. In other words, what we believe shapes our realities. My first introduction to this concept that beliefs determine what we experience came from Harry Palmer's work. In his book *Living Deliberately*, he says, "When we perceive that the only difference between any of us is beliefs, and that beliefs can be created or discreated with ease, the right and wrong game will wind down, and world peace will ensue." Having this ability to manage our beliefs, to not only decide to believe something but to also stop believing something, could be one of the greatest advances in human consciousness.

At twenty-six, I learned a lot about my beliefs as they were challenged daily when I moved to Osaka, Japan, as a bartender. I was plopped right into the middle of the Buddhist and Shinto Japanese religions and many thousands of years-old social customs, throwing my Caucasian, Ohioan, Lutheran upbringing for a loop. In Japan, simple things like not wearing shoes indoors, respect for elders, and the fact that horse and whale are delicacies all had me feeling like a deer in headlights. But I loved it! Every minute was new, a new experience, a new perspective. It was an adventure a minute. However, being exposed to that much unknown, I started to question my beliefs.

For nearly nine years, in order to learn the Japanese language, I rode my bicycle thirty minutes, three times a week, to a wise, widowed Japanese woman's house on the outskirts of town to study. In her Zen-like home, Sensei, as I called her, told me many stories, but two about letting go of beliefs have stayed with me.

The first is called "Saiou ga uma." The full title is "Ningen banji, Saiou ga uma," a rough translation being "All human affairs are like old man Sai's horse." This is my version:

An old farmer named Sai was tending his fields when his favorite horse got loose and ran away. All the villagers said, "Oh, that's too bad." Sai smiled and said, "It is what it is." A few days later, his horse came back with a beautiful mare in tow. "Oh, that's so great!" the villagers exclaimed. Sai smiled and said, "It is what it is." A few days later, when trying to tame the mare, Sai's son fell off the horse and broke his leg. "Oh, too bad," said the villagers. "It is what it is," replied Sai. While his son was still healing, the army came through town and took all the young men to war. Of course, Sai's son was not able to go because of his leg. "So lucky for you," said the villagers. Sai smiled and said...

You get the idea. For me, Sai's "It is what it is" translates to, "Yep, I **get to** experience this too."

The second story Sensei told me is this:

A young monk was peacefully walking through the jungle. A tiger appeared and started after him. The young monk ran, laughing, knowing this could be the end. Just as the tiger was about to pounce on him, the monk grabbed a vine and started climbing up the side of a cliff. He was half-way up, still laughing, when he saw above him another tiger gnawing at the vine at the top of the cliff, the original tiger hungrily waiting below. A moment later, the young monk noticed a red, ripe strawberry growing next to where he was hanging. With a huge smile, he reached out, tenderly took it off the vine, and slowly took a bite.

Living in the state of mind like Sai and the young monk is, well, *utopian* in how unrealistic it is for most of us. However, it is something to aspire to, a state of mind where your beliefs are suspended, you smile and say, "I get to experience this," and you taste the red, ripe strawberry of life.

Below are two lists. On the left are Get To thoughts and on the right are Victim thoughts. What I want you to do is read the Get To thoughts first, straight down,

and then pause. How do you feel? Is that who you want to be?

Next, read the Victim thoughts. How do you feel? Is that who you want to be?

GET TO thoughts	**VICTIM** thoughts
Be grateful	Take things for granted
Receive graciously	Criticize others
Have compassion	Hold others in contempt
Want others to succeed	Secretly hope others fail
Extend favors to others	Blame others for failures
Take inspired action	Fear change
Be courageous	Take the easy way
Embrace happiness and joy	Feel disappointment
Be curious	Have a set viewpoint
Have appreciation	Exude anger
Forgive everyone including yourself	Hold grudges
Have positive thoughts	Be bored
Have confidence	Blame circumstances for your life
Feel peace	Feel overwhelmed

The most common response I get after asking people how they feel after reading the lists is something like, "Of course I want to have Get To thoughts, but life happens. I blame, I judge, I fear. I have all kinds of thoughts and beliefs that are **out of my control**."

And there it is, "**out of my control**." Because of the speed at which our minds sling thoughts around in our skull, we think they're out of our control. And therefore, we believe *who we are* is "out of our control." It's not! We're going to look at an anomaly called "thought indulgence" in chapter 7, but for the most part, we are creators with the ability to choose what we think. Really get this, and your life will immediately change.

Saying "I *get to* experience this" (whatever you are experiencing) is the act of creating the belief that you are not a victim of life but a participant, a creator, and you can choose your next thought. I decided to learn the electric guitar a few years ago. I was fifty-two. My fingers bled, my knuckles ached, I got frustrated, and my kids and wife pretty much hated me. But I stuck with it, and now, four years later, I'm pretty good. Changing what you think is, like that, a decision. Can you take a few aches and some complaining from people if it means changing your life? Sure, it takes patience and effort, and to be fair, our everyday challenges with loss, worry, and fear can be mind-numbing. It's not easy. But for many of us, with our basic needs met, we're really just one belief, one decision, away from creating the lives of our dreams.

Believe that change is possible, and anything can change.

What do you want to experience? What goals can you get to try?

FOUR
STEPPING INTO THE EMERGING FUTURE

As you begin observing yourself and the stillness becomes deeper, there is yet another aspect to the Get To Principle that starts to reveal itself. The great philosopher Alan Watts observed, "The art of living… is neither careless drifting on the one hand nor fearful clinging to the past and the known on the other. It consists in being sensitive to each moment, in regarding it as utterly new and unique, in having the mind open and wholly receptive."

Enter Otto Scharmer and his Theory U work. Theory U "revolves around a core process of co-sensing and co-shaping emerging future possibilities." As we embrace the Get To Principle and become quiet with the present moment, we become aware and open to what is emerging.

Scharmer writes, "We have the gift to engage with two very different qualities and streams of time. One of them is a quality of the present moment that is basically an extension of the past. The present moment is shaped by what has been. The second is a quality of the present moment that functions as a gateway to a field of future possibilities. The present moment is shaped by what is wanting to emerge."

Applying the Get To mantra with an emphasis on what wants to emerge in your life, creating what author Joseph Jaworski calls "predictable miracles," will change how you experience what arises. Get To, smile, experience the emerging future.

We are on a continuous journey of waking up to

this emergence. It's a moment-to-moment choice to feel not just a state of peace at the beauty all around but an intuitive sense of what is coming. In the book *Presence: An Exploration of Profound Change in People, Organizations, and Society*, Peter Senge and several colleagues tell of how Jonas Salk, the inventor of the polio vaccine, attributed his success in developing that life-saving drug to "tapping into the continually unfolding 'dynamism' of the universe, and experiencing its evolution."

This state brought on by living Get To, by applying it at every turn in your life, is something we all strive for. That is, to not be stuck in the past or be worried about an imagined future. To live fully, freely, and with wild abandon in the present moment, with the un-thought-about emerging future literally at our fingertips. Do you want to create a new life, a new business, a new way of being? Dive in!

PART THREE

HOW TO CREATE YOUR PERFECT LIFE

"LIFE ISN'T ABOUT FINDING YOURSELF. LIFE IS ABOUT CREATING YOURSELF."
—PAULO COELHO

FIVE
YOU GET TO CREATE

As you say "I get to" throughout the day, as your step is a little lighter and maybe you're whistling just a little more, a feeling often arises. The feeling of "I want to create." We are all creative, whether our creativity is demonstrated through a hobby we're working on, a job we're involved in, being creative in our relationships, or even raising our kids. As you live Get To, no longer a victim to life but in the flow of life, you automatically *create*. Talking new initiatives with your boss? Creative.

Planning a trip or a date with your spouse? Creative. Fixing breakfast? Setting a fancy table? Playing or doing crafts with your kids? It's all creative.

The creative process is important to understand, and it is at the core of living Get To. Heck, the creative process is at the core of living, period. In fact, you can start creating now in two simple stages.

Stage 1: The Idea and Creative Concept Stage

In her book *Big Magic*, Elizabeth Gilbert speaks of how she believes creativity comes from ideas and that ideas are "disembodied, energetic life forms" floating all around us, just waiting for a human to take them on and bring them to life. She says it's magical, that the creativity that comes from ideas is a "force of enchantment." I love that. I'd never really thought of where ideas come from. I mean, you just have ideas, right? But ideas do come from somewhere, and since I didn't have a better explanation, I've loosely adapted Liz's philosophy, picturing ideas as invisible seeds floating around, looking for a place to be planted, nourished, and grown.

Here's the thing. Once an "idea seed" comes to you, you get to act on it. If you don't, it will find someone else to bring it to life. I know people who have had incredible ideas that came from, as they would say, "God knows where," but they never did anything with them. The problem is, they didn't have the "Get To, smile, create" fertile state of mind. Like I did when the portable screen door idea visited me...

In 1986, I was living in a one-bedroom apartment in Reno, Nevada. I was doing a two-year stint bartending at the MGM Grand Casino and, yada, yada, yada, drugs, sex, and rock and roll (but that's another story). Anyway, the apartment, one of hundreds of similar units in the complex, had a front metal door that opened to a long, covered outdoor hallway, and in the back, a living room sliding door with a sliding screen that opened to an open field. In the spring and summer, although it might be breezy and cool outside, it was often stuffy and hot inside.

One hot day when I came home from grocery shopping and entered through the front door, a sweet, cool breeze followed me in. I had many times, like thousands of other people over the years in those apartments, come through the front door, felt the cool breeze...and promptly closed the door to keep the bugs out.

But this time, I stopped and stood. I was in a very creative mood, and an idea seed planted in my brain. I propped the door open with the bag of groceries, walked to the living room, and opened the back door. It was as if I turned on the AC. Bugs be damned, I thought. The idea landed and started to sprout. **What if** I put a screen on the front door? Nah, too much hassle to install, and besides, it's a rental. But **what if** I had a spring-loaded, detachable, inexpensive, *portable* screen door? The idea grew, and I looked around. Hundreds of the same apartment units, no screen doors. I looked farther. Hundreds of apartment complexes in Reno with hundreds of units each—with no screen doors. Millions of doors across America in need of a portable screen door that renters could install, *click click*, take out, *snap snap*, and take with them. The idea seed had been there, and I let it in.

From there, I began my quest to bring that idea to life. I didn't know any official, formal steps to the

creative process; I just did them. For me, it didn't need to be complicated. I studied and researched (there was nothing like it in the market), and I suppose in there, it somehow illuminated, incubated, valuated, and implemented. But really, I just bought materials and made various mock-ups. I had a blast working on it, putting it together. I moved from Reno to San Diego, where I continued to bartend (at the San Diego Chargers football games and then the Sheraton Grand Hotel) and worked on the idea that had so willingly come to me. And eventually, I had a prototype portable screen door. Ta-da!

Creating really is as simple as saying "Get To, smile, create." As you maintain that "I create" mindset, you become a fertile garden for the idea seeds floating around. What if? becomes a common question you ask at everything you see. What if I put a rock in a box and sold it as a pet? (Pet rocks sold 1.4 million units in 1975.) What if I put a smiley face on a T-shirt? What if I take this spring and call it a Slinky. What if?

There are many courses and gurus offering complicated ideas on how to be creative. It's fine to look at them and see how they might assist you, but don't get too caught up with the jargon. Just repeat the mantra "Get To, smile, create," then ask **what if**, and the idea seeds will come calling.

Stage 2: The Share, Succeed, Sell Stage

If you're happy with stage 1, then *celebrate*. Love it. If the idea that came to me had been a painting for my mom, planting a unique garden, or the design of my daughter's gymnastics stage act for her third grade talent show, perfect. Done. Set the creation free, and get yourself ready for the next inspiration.

However, if your creation calls for a bigger audience, stage 2 is your next step. But beware, it's this stage where millions of ideas are squandered, left out to dry, and as we so often hear, "never see the light of day." Like the portable screen door, many of our ideas are meant to be made and sold or otherwise shared with the world. The idea is meant to be brought out to bask in the glory of its evolution into what it has become. But many ideas don't come to fruition, and that is the end of the line, the death of that creativity. Because it was meant to be seen, heard, felt, tasted, used, read, or otherwise experienced by many but wasn't, our consciousness sighs a collective "too bad"

and instructs the idea seed to move on and find the next fertile mind.

As we begin to bring our ideas to a larger audience, our beliefs in our abilities, our confidence in the idea, our self-esteem, and our willpower take a beating from the outside. Friends and family say, "Who are you to do that?" "Get a real job." "That's nice, honey, but how's your resume coming along?" I got lucky and didn't have too much of that chatter from friends and family responding to my cockamamie ideas through life, but I didn't need them. I had resistance yelling at me, screaming, "You can't do it!" "You suck!" "Your dad's a janitor. Why do you think you can do better than that?" Also, like everyone, ego, at resistance's side, inflated me one moment but sucked the wind out of me and spit me out the next. It's a roller coaster.

Do you want to take the next step in an endeavor you're in? Sell something you've created? Get in shape, be a better parent, get over call reluctance, and *create*? What is it for you? No matter how much you try, do you often fail to complete it because resistance and ego are blaring their horns in your head? There is only one way to combat these forces—taking action.

SIX

YOU GET TO
TAKE ACTION

As I'm writing this, on New Year's Day 2019, millions of people around the world have made New Year's resolutions: "I'll lose weight," "I'll exercise more," "I'll make more money," "I'll learn a new language," "I'll play with my kids more," "I'll quit smoking," "I'll sell my big idea."

Many of us (dare I say most) will *not* achieve our goals. We have the idea, we prepare (gym membership secured, latest get-rich-quick seminar on the laptop, the quit-smoking nicotine patches on our arms) and, like a wet firework, our plan soon fizzles. We do well for a while, and then it slowly fades, and we're back to our daily routine. Notice how I say *we*. Yeah, I've known as well as anyone the drill of hoping to affect change in my life and not doing it. Except now I know a way, a way most people don't know exists.

As you may have gathered, I'm a fan of new age thinking and the human potential movement overall. Along with playing with beliefs to change your experience, I think vision boards, mantras, chanting, meditating, yoga, and putting Post-it Notes on my bathroom mirror saying "I'm a millionaire" or "I'm a rock star" are awesome to explore and motivate. However, I'm going to share an aspect I believe is missing from all that. A way of approaching the "becoming who I want to be" mindset that will drive you to action.

To start, when it comes to making changes in life, you need to be clear on where you are at this moment. You need a true sense of **current reality**. You also need a clear idea of what you want to create with a vision of a future reality based on tapping into your **true self**. You see, if you don't look deeply with astute awareness, really look at what's going on, fundamental change can be tough. Yes, changing one belief could do it, and meditating with crystals in bowls of salt water all around you might help, but the complex human psyche often needs *more*. Especially when it comes to tackling addictions, which New Year's resolutions most often try to overcome. The key is looking at the **underlying structural dynamic** of what is happening and allowing change to happen naturally.

I am going to use losing weight as an example to explore further, since many of us ride this roller coaster within our goals of being healthier. Eating too much of the wrong stuff and being a couch potato are so ubiquitous in our society that it's easy for most of us to relate to such behavior. But please know this could be about harder addictions, such as drinking alcohol, doing drugs, watching porn, or cheating on your partner, or

about softer addictions, such as working too much, watching too much TV, scrolling through social media too long, or the *underachieving* or *overindulging in anything* that makes us feel like crap afterward.

To start, there's a deep part of everyone (yes, you too) that wants more than the surface clinging we do for things. Oprah says, "Your authentic self is that part of you that longs for more than just possessions or temporary pleasures." I'm going to say that again, because this is so fundamental to change: "Your authentic self is that part of you that longs for more than just possessions or temporary pleasures." When you access your authentic self, your true self, a new structure is put in place, and the game of Get To take action begins.

Let me define underlying structural dynamic. If you simply said, "Yippee, I want to lose weight," and you lost fifty pounds and never put it back on, that would be one thing. But when you say "I want to lose weight" and you sigh, and then struggle...and then don't, there's something **underlying** those "I want to lose weight" words. Maybe struggles to get food as a kid, or the emotional pain that eating covered up as a teen, or current stress eating that developed in response to what's happening at work. Whatever it is, it's a **dynamic** (complex) structure of your mind that is sabotaging what you are working to create...in this case, losing weight.

So, for our example, here's the old **underlying structural dynamic**: You say, "I want to lose weight." What you're trying to do, the structure of your mind, **is solve a problem**: having too much weight. It really doesn't matter what caused it (from childhood trauma, DNA, or otherwise); it's simply the structure in place. The other problem, the **unspoken problem**, is that you're bad to have so much weight in the first place.

But you promise yourself, "This time, I'm going to change." You cram the fridge with all the salad fixings, hire a personal trainer, and get to it. At first, you feel pretty good. You lose a few pounds, and you're consistent with workouts. Why, you're not so bad after all! As you get comfortable over a few weeks or even a few months, the perceived conflict, losing weight and being a bad person, is resolved, and motivation to continue weakens. You miss a few workouts and sneak in a Twinkie. You tell yourself, "No big deal. I got this." But you start to feel guilt, which sets up more conflict, and the old pattern of breaking promises to yourself translates to "I am a weak loser who can't even make it to the gym to support my own health and well-being," which leads to some form of "What's the use? Turn on *The Good Place* and give me that Snickers bar." Ever feel that way? Trust me, I've had plenty of Snickers bars in response to life.

Obviously, that's a structure that has failed all of us over and over. Ready to change? True creating is not about solving a problem. Instead, you think in terms of a new underlying structure, focusing on who you want to be, not what you want to change. It's moving from a place where your **tendencies are governing you** to a

place where you're observing, retreating, and reflecting, and from a new viewpoint, you're able to make changes to reach and maintain your goal.

It's about **creating** what you desire from a state of excitement. Creating is bringing something into existence that didn't exist before—**out of love**. As the YouTuber Lilly Singh says, "Love who you are, embrace who you are. Love yourself." Problem solving is getting rid of something not wanted. Demolition, not architecture. *We Get To be architects of our lives!*

You don't have to be a better person. You're fine exactly as you are. It's a matter of creating your aspirations, which is the highest expression of the human spirit. You don't have to work on you; you are simply working on the creation—the structure. You change the narrative from "I have a problem and want to lose weight" to "My true self wants to be healthy. My true self, deep in my heart, loves this life, and I create great health. I will take action that aligns with that." *The commitment to be in service to what YOU really*

want, what YOU desire—that's the essence of making true change.

With that clarification, a sense of purpose is created, driving you from the current state to the desired state. It's a tension that, by nature, wants to resolve to completion. The idea of creating purpose that drives creativity is defined nicely by Robert Fritz in the book *The Path of Least Resistance*. His central theme is what he calls "structural tension," and he says "the power of structural tension…is that the difference between the desired state and the actual state creates a powerful state of 'non-equilibrium' that has a built-in dynamic, to restore equilibrium."

Once you decide "My true self wants to be healthy," and you identify clearly where you are now, without judgment of it being a problem, tension is created, and you naturally move up in that direction. When you look at a piece of cake, you can feel the urge, but because you have awareness of the new structure of wanting to create as opposed to solving a problem, the tension naturally pulls you up toward what your **true self wants to experience**. You can observe and say, "Oh, there's the old structure at play. I feel the urge, but I'm on a different path in life, and I'm not going to eat it." **That's creating!**

It's important to note that we're not getting rid of the urge; we're acknowledging it. The new way of thinking, the new structure allows us to move toward

the change we want. In the beginning, we may act on the urge, but because we're creating, not problem-solving, we observe that action, don't beat ourselves up, recommit, and take the next step in creating who we want to be.

This is an energizing dynamic, a powerful approach to life. It's one that I have adapted and fused with what I've learned about beliefs, meditating, using Post-it Notes, and being open to the emerging future. *I Get To do all those things and be a true creator of my life.*

Oh, as for my portable screen door? Remember that? Yeah, at the time, I looked at selling as a problem for me to solve, not an opportunity to create. I just didn't know. The idea seed soon left me, and by the time I learned what I'm writing about now, it was too late. Years later, I saw portable screen doors for sale at Home Depot.

SEVEN
ENDING THOUGHT INDULGENCE

Applying the Get To Principle in my everyday life has been a lifesaver, constantly bringing me back to compassion and gratitude and into the present moment. We've discussed how being in control of your thoughts and choosing Get To thoughts over Victim thoughts is a key to creating. However, there are times when no matter what we do—repeating the Get To mantra, meditating, writing out an action plan, making a vision board, chanting, stating true-self intentions, *whatever*—our minds are a whirlwind of thoughts that we feel we can't stop. Have you had that experience? Times when your thoughts are so out of control that you can't seem to get anything done? This is beyond the random wandering that our minds usually do. This is thinking on *overdrive*, usually about one particular subject, over and over and over.

I recognized this as a phenomenon, almost a sickness, we all have at times. I call it **thought indulgence**. This is an incessant thought or thoughts, beyond everyday thinking, focusing on one particular idea that repeats in your head. Thoughts of losing everything. Thoughts of winning everything. It's a conversation you plan to have later with your spouse, child, or boss that plays over and over in your mind. **Thought indulgence** is one of—if not the most—paralyzing functions of the human mind. Eckhart Tolle says, "Here's a new spiritual practice for you: don't take your thoughts too seriously." Good luck with that when you are experiencing thought indulgence.

To indulge means "to treat with unearned favor" or, more simply, "to give in to something." When we give in to these ceaseless thoughts, when we allow them to run amok, we're allowing the mind to control not only how we are but who we are and what we are creating. How? By its incessant desire to indulge in whatever it's thinking at the moment.

A thought indulgence can be either positive or negative. We can indulge in thoughts we're going to be rich and famous or indulge in thoughts that feel like they'll make us go insane.

As I was writing my first book, a self-published memoir titled *Get To Be Happy*, and as positive reviews to the manuscript started coming in from friends and family (yep, those "real" reviews), my thought indulgence of selling a million copies, being on *The Ellen DeGeneres Show*, getting rich and famous, and being on easy street almost bankrupted me. I allowed my rich thoughts to run amok. My ego mind was a wild beast of continuous thinking of an imaginary future, sitting

happily ever after at the end of the utopian rainbow, hugging my pot of gold.

What's the big deal with wanting more? Simply this: I lost focus. I didn't do the work necessary, with clarity, to succeed as a writer. There was no tension created between actual reality and where I wanted to go. I lost sight of where I was. The emerging future was shadowed by the all-consuming thought indulgence.

I was smug and spent hours in self-grandiose planning for my television debut that didn't come. I didn't listen to experts who told me again and again, "Do not plan to make money from your first book." For every J. K. Rowling who sells boatloads on her first try (and even then, it took her seven years before she made a single English pound), there are many millions of other writers who struggle to sell just a few copies. Sure, I had written a book, a damn good book, but I was still one of the millions, and I let my thought indulgence go on and on.

Six months after self-publishing and selling just a few thousand copies, the thought indulgence turned negative, as fears of ending up on the street swirled unchecked inside my fragile cranium. How can the Get To guy go from being on top of the world to sleepless nights, worrying about how I was going to make this whole thing work out? Thought indulgence—allowing my mind to focus on thoughts of fame and riches and then, when that didn't pan out, to flip to thoughts of fear and shame.

Although it can happen anytime and anywhere, negative thought indulgence often happens in the middle of the night. We wake up, and our thoughts kick into gear. It can be about anything, but the mind loves to focus on one of four areas: something I should have done, something I shouldn't have done, something I should have said, and something I shouldn't have said. Around that one event (a contract going south, a fight with my wife or kid, an upset at the office), I create stories, scenarios, conversations, and strategies on how I should have handled it. The thoughts go on and on, loop in circles, and end up nowhere. Does this sound familiar?

The beauty is that once I recognized thought indulgence for what it was, a phenomenon of our minds, I was able to apply Get To and started taking control of my life. You can do this too. I have developed a strategy, if not a cure, for dealing with thought indulgence:

FIRST: As soon as you realize you are stuck in

a thought about something, when it's repeating itself over and over, remember to use the Get To mantra by saying "Get To, smile, have that thought." Repeat this several times. Just this simple thing will stop the thought in its tracks.

SECOND: Ask yourself, "Is this a thought I want to indulge in? Is it something that I really want to put my mind on?" This puts you immediately in the driver's seat of life. In that instant, you are no longer a victim to that thought stream. You are observing it, and it becomes a choice. Your mind quiets.

THIRD: Imagine in your mind a folder, and name it "Won't happen." (You can call the folder anything, but since I've discovered 99.9% of my thought-indulgence thoughts never come true, I call it "Won't happen.") Put the thought in the folder. *OK. Phew. I feel a little calmer.* This works.

The thought may slip out of the folder at first, but you'll catch it and put it back in, and eventually it will stay there.

FOURTH: Now that the thought is no longer repeating, be grateful for and focus on the positive aspects of the situation. After this you may be able to move into experiencing the quality of the emerging future where you are free and moving forward. You'll probably go back to sleep.

Recognizing thought indulgence, stepping outside of yourself, and watching it can bring so much relief and joy. This isn't about changing the world; it's about changing how you look at the world so you react differently. **How you look at the world is how you treat it.** *How you treat the world is what the world becomes for you.*

EIGHT
BE LIKE YODA

When I was in my twenties, as Get To was percolating in my subconscious, I attended a self-development course in San Francisco. On the second day, as the fifteen of us were all heading out for lunch, the course instructor, Roy, asked us to be back promptly at 2:00 p.m. As I was walking toward the door, I looked back and said that I had a business phone call during lunch but that I would try to be back on time. In that moment, he almost yelled to everyone, "Stop what you're doing."

The bustle of getting out of chairs, picking up purses and jackets, and shuffling toward the door froze. He quietly looked at me and said in a calm voice, "Ted, put your hand on this desk."

It was silent as everyone looked at me. I shyly put my hand on the desk as he had asked, fingers splayed out as though I were in kindergarten, ready to make a turkey outline from my hand.

"Ted," he said, "try to lift your index finger."

I knew that lifting your ring finger can be a challenge, but this was a no-brainer. I lifted it.

"No," he said, "that's lifting it. Put it back down."

I did.

"Now try to lift it."

I let an embarrassing chuckle escape as I again lifted my finger.

Again, calmly, everyone's attention rapt on us, he said, "No, that's doing it. I'm asking you to try to lift your finger. Go ahead."

I was confused. I just didn't get it. I lifted it.

He looked at me once more and pointedly said, "That's doing it."

I put my finger down, and when my eyes met his, he smiled. In that moment, a light bulb went off. It was silent.

When he said again, "Please try," I didn't move. In the quiet, I could hear in my mind the "Yeah but…" wanting to scream from my lungs. I could feel a lifetime of excuses, noncommitments, and letting others down. All because I said "I'll try." I remembered the people to whom I said "I'll try" in a state of limbo, not knowing the truth of my intentions. In that moment, my hand resting on a table in a hotel conference room in San Francisco, my life changed forever. Yoda said it first, and we need to embrace and live it: "Do or do not. There is no try."

The problem is we say "try" with the same **indoctrinated ease** we say "have to." It's a habit most of us carry with us and don't even recognize we do. Ready to change? Get an accountability partner.

One of the most powerful tools in my Get To toolbox came years ago when I attended a T. Harv Eker "Millionaire Mind" seminar. Harv wrote the bestselling book *Secrets of the Millionaire Mind*. I love that book, and the weekend seminar was fun. From the stage, Harv would tell the three hundred plus people every few hours, "Turn to the person next to you and say, 'You're amazing!'" I would turn to whoever was next to me, give them a high five, and yell, "You're amazing!" In fact, it felt amazing and got me all pumped up, and at least for a few hours, I believed that I was going to be rich.

Although I didn't get rich, something powerful did come out of it. At one point, instead of the "you're amazing" drill, Harv asked us to find an accountability partner. I didn't know what that was, but in the spirt of things, I thought, why not? One of the people I was attending with, Jill, was standing next to me, and I turned and asked, "Wanna do it?"

"Whatever it is," she said, "I'm all in."

An accountability partner, as it turns out, is someone you share your goals with, and they hold you accountable to what you say you are going to do. Jill and I decided that every Monday, we would write our goals for the week and send them to each other. On the following Sunday, we would update those goals, noting what we did or didn't do. For the last eight years, without fail, every Monday, I've been sending

Jill my goals for the week. Every Sunday, without fail, I send an update.

It's easy to put it off, forget, or otherwise not do goals. But with an accountability partner, there are no excuses, and **there are no trys**. Vacation, business trips, or just plain busy, we do it. And if one of us is late, the other will say, "What the hell? Are you OK? Have you been in a car accident? Because if not, your goals are late, and that's not OK." But that's rarely the case, because we now call them our Get To goals and have that attitude toward the process. There is no try; we do. And that permeates our lives. Much as I no longer say "I have to," I no longer say "I'll try."

Get an accountability partner. Or get a coach. A main function of my coaching practice is to hold my clients accountable. They set intentions, state goals, and write them down, and we review them weekly. They do, and sometimes they don't do, but they're clear on their path in life and moving forward—not *trying* to.

NINE

THE MAGIC OF THE $10 MILLION MINDSET

This tool is the epitome of powerful creating through Get To.

I was on my weekly call with my coaching partner, John Davidson, and we were discussing my then-current role as senior vice president for DHX Media's licensing division, CPLG, in Hollywood. He asked what my financial goals were for my group. "Well," I said, "the top brass are expecting $3 million in sales from us. I'm thinking my goal is going to be $3.2 million."

JD was quiet. It got uncomfortable. Still silent. I nervously laughed. It was just the two of us on our weekly phone call, so I'm not sure why I was nervous. Oh, because I knew in my heart I was playing it safe! Duh!

"OK," I said. "I'll make my goal $4 million!" That was a lot above the expected $3 million, and I felt good. No nervous laughing now. But JD remained silent.

"What?" I asked. "OK, $5 million." He remained silent. In the quiet, my heart started racing. It started to beat faster, and I could feel it in my chest as I finally blurted out, almost yelled, "$10 million! That's my goal, goddamn it!" I could hear JD smile. I smiled.

The next morning in the budget meeting with my team, I used the same tactic JD used with me. "So, what do you think our target should be?" They each mumbled something in the $3 million range. They weren't stupid: whatever number you give the corporate bean counters, you know they'll come back asking for more regardless, and once you agree to a number, you've got twelve months to produce that money or risk being fired. Life in the corporate world!

It was quiet for a minute, and I decided to dive in. "Our number for the year is $10 million."

The raised eyebrows. The dropped jaws. The "What the hell do you mean?" stares. Erin said, "There's no way we can generate that much in sales this year. And if you report it and we don't hit that number, we're goners."

I explained the incredible realization I had had the day before. In her book *You Are a Badass*, Jen Sincero says, "Act as if you're where you want to be. Erase the words 'I can't' from your vocabulary. Envision what you desire. Set goals. And demand of yourself that you become who you need to become to create the life you desire." This last sentence, the theme throughout our journey here, was it: ***become who you need to become to create the life you desire***. Jen also ends each of her chapters with "Love yourself." Yes!

"Guys," I said, "I'm not going to report this to

corporate. This is **our** number. The exercise is, 'Who do we need to become to create $10 million?' Can you see, with this viewpoint, that we'll quit quibbling over the $2,000 deals? We'll choose the accounts that are more difficult to close but that generate ten times the revenue. We'll wake up energized and excited with the prospect of actually creating $10 million in sales. The question is, will you do your part to make this happen as a team? Are you willing to go for $10 million?"

They shuffled and started to awaken: Who do we need to become to create $10 million? We called it the **$10 million mindset**. One person said excitedly, "We **Get To** create $10 million!" We laughed. We submitted $3.5 million to the bean counters.

We had fun with it, in every meeting asking what we were doing to create $10 million in sales. We looked at each contract or time-sucking client, deciding if it was in alignment with creating $10 million. Brian and Elliot suggested doing a daily afternoon walk around Hollywood to brainstorm $10 million ideas. We did and came up with some great concepts. We used structural tension to build strategies, we used Get To in order to have appreciation for our work, and we tapped into the emerging future to intuit what was even possible. Over the next number of months, we did pretty well, our sales increasing, but not, and not surprisingly, to the $10 million level. It didn't matter. We were having fun. We were creating. We were becoming who we knew we could be.

Then the magic happened. One day, I got a call from my boss, Peter. "Ted," he said, "I want to give you a heads-up that DHX will be announcing the purchase of the *Peanuts* brand. Snoopy, Charlie Brown, the whole thing. The purchase price is $345 million." Of course, I had known the deal was in the works, but I wasn't really involved. At first, I was just happy for the company and the influx of business opportunities it represented. But a moment later, I realized what it meant. I hadn't figured it out until that moment. The sales of Snoopy product in the United States, my territory, were nearly

$40 million. Our $10 million mindset had worked—times four!

It was magic. I realized that we were part of something bigger than making our numbers at the office. By deliberately having a $10 million mindset, you tap into this vast energy that is available to all of us, all of the time.

Think about your next project and apply the $10 million mindset. If your project is $10 million already, make it the $100 million mindset. Play. Have fun. Create!

PART
FOUR

LIVING
THE GET TO
LIFE

"BEING STILL IS A SUPERPOWER."
—WILL SMITH

TEN

GET TO LISTEN TO OTHERS

We, as humans, are who we are not in spite of but because of other people. You may grow up and decide to be a hermit in a cave, but unless you popped out and grew up by yourself in the jungle (if you're reading this, you didn't), you started out fully immersed with others, and you became who you are in relation to everyone you've met to this moment. Everyone you meet today will help define who you are tomorrow.

When I was a teenager, I said to someone, "You're

awesome." The reply has stuck with me ever since: **"I can only be who I am as a reflection in the mirror of you."**

Desmond Tutu said, "We would not know how to think, or walk, or speak, or behave as human beings unless we learned it from other human beings... I am because other people are."

However, as important as being connected with others is, we have become more and more isolated, stuck in our own worlds, not willing or able to **truly connect** with people. Hiding behind our electronic devices doesn't help, but I think there is a more fundamental source of the problem: not being able to listen. We all enjoy our solitude at times, but in the quest for that solitude, our abilities to connect, to be present, and, most of all, to listen have faded.

Relationship is the organizing principle of the universe. Everything is intertwined and connected. Once we embrace this, we realize that everyone we meet, even the beggars on the exit ramps, are messengers, each with something to give us that can change the direction of our lives. We can see the most incredible sunset, look out over majestic mountains, and be in awe, but one eye exchange with another human, one simple conversation, is precious beyond words. Antoine de Saint-Exupéry, the author of *The Little Prince*, wrote that **"Those who pass by us, do not go alone, and do not leave us alone; they leave a bit of themselves, and take a little of us."**

To truly connect with people, we need to listen. I have identified three stages to listening. As you become aware of these three stages while you are with people, you will automatically begin to hear and connect on a deeper level. Relationships will begin to have more meaning.

Stage 1: Not Listening

We all know this feeling. A person is talking, and you barely hear a word they're saying. You may have a point to make and are just waiting your turn to talk. You simply may not be interested or have another pressing matter you want to attend to and are just biding your time. But most often, you're just lost in your own thoughts about life. Nothing against the person speaking, but you're just not clicked in. You're just not there.

Stage 2: Shifting to Active Listening

When you recognize you aren't listening, you start to wake up. "Oops, I'm not hearing a word they're saying." In that moment, you can stop them and say, "Sorry to interrupt, but I have another matter to attend to. Love ya, see ya, bye" (as my kids would say). Or refocus your attention on the person and begin to listen. "I'm sorry, I got lost in thought. Can you say that again?" is an honest and respectful way to move into this stage. At this point, you are in **active listening** and are engaged with the other person.

Stage 3: Immersion in the Conversation

As you start **listening** on a deeper level, you naturally become more interested in not just what is being said but in what wants to emerge. You are fully engaged in the conversation, and your genuine engagement will invite the other to fully engage as well. You are applying "Get To, smile, listen." You are fully immersed in the conversation. You are connected. Predictable miracles appear. A sense of tapping into what is coming from the future begins to develop, and true creativity starts to unfold.

As you go about your day, remain aware of these three stages. Recognize when you are **not listening**. Don't judge; just be with it. In reality, the person who's speaking may be on crack and out of their mind, so it might be good to stay disconnected and not go any deeper.

However, if it's your eleven-year-old telling you about her day at school, you might want to wake up and start **listening**. "Sorry, honey, say that again" and

get down to her level and begin to **actively listen**. Listening might be enough with your daughter. It often is with mine.

But what if you're in a conversation with your spouse about, let's say, selling the house and moving to another state? Yep, I was in a conversation with my wife, Beth, about a pending move, and I was not present. We were talking about selling our house, and

I was thinking about visiting my friend Pat in Tampa! It was not pretty. But then I remembered Get To, I got present, started actively listening, and soon fell into an immersion as we strategized our next move, creating into the emerging future.

Be aware, go deeper, and have appreciation. Be the co-creator of what is emerging from the conversation. You become part of the collective whole, participating in life on a deeper level, bringing into the world what is wanting to emerge. This is where magic happens. It's pretty cool.

We are not alone on the planet. As the saying goes: *"How you see people is how you treat them. How you treat them is who they become."* Look at people, smile, and connect. Immerse yourself with them. Become this world we are creating together.

ELEVEN
PERSISTENCE AND RESISTANCE

If you haven't read Napoleon Hill's book *Think and Grow Rich*, please do! It's a brilliant piece of work and will alter how you view the world and your ability to live a Get To life. It was the beginning of the positive thinking movement and remains as relevant now as it was then.

In it, Hill shares the story of how a man named R. U. Darby and his uncle had gold rush fever, bought a piece of land, and after a few hard weeks with a pick and shovel, found some gold. With this news, they went to friends and family and secured money to buy machinery. They went back and had great luck mining more gold, enough to pay back the loans. But then the gold ran out. They dug and drilled a little farther but to no avail. They decided to quit and sold everything to a junk man for a few hundred dollars. The junk man did a little looking and found, three feet farther from where Darby and his uncle had stopped, a massive gold mine worth millions of dollars.

The moral of the story, of course, is never give up. Never stop. After all the believing, the creative thinking, the tensioning, the meditating, and of course the Get To-ing, everything comes down to one thing: **persistence**. Just keep going. Here's the definition: "the fact of continuing in an opinion or course of action *in spite of difficulty* or opposition." Don't quit. Here's the definition of the cousin of persistence, **perseverance**: "to remain patient and attentive, especially during a lengthy or problematic situation that may cause one to want to quit or leave prematurely."

As someone once wrote, "Nothing in this world can take the place of persistence. Talent will not; nothing is more common than unsuccessful men with talent. Genius will not; unrewarded genius is almost a proverb. Education will not; the world is full of educated derelicts. Persistence and determination alone are omnipotent."

The sad thing about giving up is that unlike Mr. Darby, who soon found out what gold he missed, rarely will you know what was lying just around the bend. You'll never know how close you were. It's easy to throw in the towel, raise the white flag, drop out, surrender, cede, abandon, capitulate, give in, **say uncle**. I know I've used all those terms at some point in my life, sometimes while on my knees crying. We do it because we don't know how close we are.

I've come to realize that it is rare that you need to give up. It's just our minds playing tricks on us, our egos saying, "Here, let me handle it. Hmmm, let's see. Nah, too tough. Let's stop." We buy into it. We see the greener field, the shinier penny, the more attractive job/woman/man/diet/get-rich-quick program, stop what we're doing, and move to the next thing. We tell ourselves, OK, the next one will be it. Or we say it's too hard. Or not worth it. Or it's not really what we wanted in the first place.

Where is all this coming from? In his fabulous book *The War of Art*, Steven Pressfield attributes giving up to an outside force, something almost living called **resistance**. He says that "resistance cannot be seen, touched, heard, or smelled. But it can be felt. We experience it as an energy field radiating from a work-in-potential. It's a repelling force. It's negative. Its aim is to shove us away, distract us, prevent us from doing our work."

Resistance works closely with our egos and joins the echoes in our minds saying, "Nah, let's just quit." **Don't do it.** Don't let resistance stop you. My grandfather, Richard C. Larkins, was athletic director of Ohio State University. He hired the famous (infamous?) football coach Woody Hayes who, through much controversy (punching an opposing team's player in the face was just a bit controversial), helped make the Ohio State Buckeyes one of the best college football teams in the country. You know what Woody said? "Paralyze resistance with persistence."

The Little Engine That Could didn't say, "I think I can, I think I can, I think I…I…can't." No way. That could have been a much shorter—or longer—story, but we knew how it was going to turn out in the end. Are you trying to lose weight? Start a business? Meditate every day? Be nice to your kids? Don't let resistance rear its ugly head; paralyze it with persistence. Make that your life. Decide right now: Get To, smile, never give up.

TWELVE

HAPPINESS IS—AND NOTHING MORE

Our forefathers got it wrong. It shouldn't be the "pursuit of happiness." It should read: "Life, liberty, and **the expansion of the happiness that's inside us**."

As Aristotle said, "Happiness is the meaning and the purpose of life, the whole aim and end of human existence."

As Anne Frank said, "We all live with the objective of being happy; our lives are all different and yet the same."

As the Dalai Lama said, "I believe the purpose of life is to be happy."

In his book *Happiness Rocks*, Ricky Powell said, "Not only is happiness readily available in any moment you choose, it can also be your springboard for creating success in every area of your life."

I could keep going, keep quoting, but the point remains the same—happiness is important for a fulfilling life. Some people say that happiness is overrated, but I don't listen. Most, like the people quoted earlier, agree it's the bedrock of a good life.

For me, the Get To Principle embodies happiness, not as some utopian life only a lucky few can obtain, but as a state of mind that is intentionally created by not being a victim to what is going on around you and having great appreciation for your life. Really, it's that simple. It's an attitude shift. Get To, smile, be happy. This is something I believe can be compounded with four simple keys to happiness.

1. Have Purpose

This isn't about finding your purpose. It's not about searching; it's about **having** purpose. Here's the difference. We've been taught a false need to "find yourself" in order to find a purpose. Most of the religious and new age teachings are all about this finding a purpose struggle. However, if you're searching, looking, or trying to find your purpose, you're missing the point of life. *Life itself is purpose.* It took me a while to get this, but when I did, I was free. Instead of searching for a purpose, *I simply had a purpose.*

This started hitting home back in the '80s when I was reading Dan Millman's book *Way of the Peaceful Warrior*. The character, Dan, had been on a mind trip, traveling through the world with the gas station attendant/veiled guru Socrates, when he proclaimed, "Everyone everywhere lived a confused, bitter search. Reality never matched their dreams; happiness was just around the corner—a corner they never turned. And the source of it all was the human mind."

It started sinking in. No searching is needed. I had purpose—just being me. I saw the things I had, the things I craved, the approval I sought, for what they were: temporary things made up in my mind. My purpose, and I believe everyone's purpose, is to simply be the best we can be. From that understanding, happiness ensues.

2. Have Compassion

Many of us walk around in a state of martyrdom. We think, "The world is in crappy condition, and we must suffer for it." We've been taught that we should "feel sorry for" or "have pity on" others. But pity, according to the dictionary, "implies slightly *contemptuous* sorrow for one in misery or distress." Are you kidding me? Stop it! Get To is about having *compassion*, "a sympathetic consciousness of other's distress together with a desire to alleviate it." Not contemptuous sorrow! This is not about having pity or feeling sorry for people. When you have compassion, you exude a natural joy and feel compelled to take action. That action might only be to share your happiness. When the oxygen mask of happiness drops, if you're able—just like in an airplane—put yours on first and then help others by sharing your joy and compassion for life. That could be all the world needs from you.

3. Be Grateful

We often feel that our present existence is lacking, that we don't have enough right now. In that state we can feel lonely and down. However, when you are grateful for the things you do have, you connect with your true self and awaken an energy within you that is filled with joy. It quiets your mind and allows you to appreciate things just as they are. It's saying yes to what is. Being grateful brings the present moment alive.

Let's do it right now. Think of three things you are grateful for. Then, repeat the mantra "Get To, smile, be grateful." I just noticed my guitar and my cat, Dreamer, laying nearby. You can even do it on a thought. I just thought of my daughter, Nia. "Get To, smile, be grateful for Nia." Ah, that made me smile. Now it's your turn. Do it several times, and you'll start to feel the shift to feeling joy.

Having gratitude is one of the easiest paths to happiness.

4. Know That Happiness Is Your Nature

Ramana Maharshi said it best: "Happiness is your nature. It is not wrong to desire it. What is wrong is seeking it outside when it is inside." The more we take time to get quiet, allow our minds to settle down, and become present, we realize that being happy is a natural state. Yes, do good work, be creative, get things, give things, be inspired, and inspire others. Really, do all of it. But please, please remember that it really is a choice, that happiness is your nature.

As good ol' Abe Lincoln said, "Folks are usually about as happy as they make up their minds to be."

You **Get To** be happy.

Ready. Set. Go!

"LEARN HOW TO BE HAPPY WITH WHAT YOU HAVE WHILE YOU PURSUE ALL THAT YOU WANT."

—JIM ROHN

ACKNOWLEDGMENTS

One day, I found myself on a call with Dominique Raccah, CEO of Sourcebooks, the largest independent, woman-led publisher in the United States. She said, "Ted, I read your book (*Get To Be Happy*) and am a Get To fan." I was stunned. Dominique is a rock star in the publishing world, and she and her team were calling *me*? I asked her how she had even seen my self-published book. "I just like to read" was her response. Luck, fate, or just a predictable miracle—it didn't matter. She had read my book, and I was psyched to be on the phone with her. She said she wanted to publish a self-help version of Get To, focusing on the power of the principle it holds, different from the memoir version I had created.

On the line was her editor, Meg Gibbons, and Dominique instructed us to make it happen. We signed a contract, and over the next eight months, Meg and I worked on the outline and then the manuscript. Meg has an incredible sense, and the seven thousand words she cut from my first draft brought out and perfectly highlighted Get To. I should probably share the billing with her. It's amazing to work with such talent. Also, thanks to Leyla Parada and Grace Menary-Winefield on the team. I'm honored to be working with such an incredible organization. Thanks also to:

Harry Palmer and the Avatar® materials. The mission of creating an Enlightened Planetary Civilization® is real, and I've enjoyed the exploration of it.

My coach and wingman on the Get To journey, John

Davidson. JD brought me into the emerging future of Get To and pulled me out of the muck of despair more than once. Without him, Get To would not be.

Diana Plattner, the editor for the original *Get To Be Happy* book, who remains a major force in its success. Bob Cashatt, who did the interior layout, and Diana are incredible partners.

David-o Brown, Pat Torrence, Andrew Lombardi, and Josiah Hargadon. They're just buds, but without them and their counsel, I'd be lost.

My sisters, Kathy and Julie, for who I became.

My wife, Beth, and kids, Will and Nia, for who I am becoming.

Lastly, and as cliché as it sounds, the Universe. As separate as I often feel from it, the truth is I am it, and when I feel that, it's pure grace and love.

ABOUT THE AUTHOR

PHOTO © SHANA MENAKER

Ted Larkins is an author, speaker, and trainer on change management and personal and executive life strategy, sharing a powerful concept he calls the Get To Principle. Ted helps individuals visualize, create, and reach major goals (personal and business) and helps companies become powerful and productive by creating empowered teams that love what they do.

Ted was a product licensing and promotional executive for over thirty years, generating over $500 million in sales of licensed products and paying clients tens of millions of dollars in royalties. During his thirty years working in Japan (nine years living in Osaka), he co-developed one of the largest entertainment licensing companies in Asia, representing Pepsi, New Balance, and many of the Hollywood movie studios, including Paramount Pictures, Sony Pictures, MGM, Twentieth Century Fox, and DreamWorks. Ted represented and negotiated deals for many artists, including Audrey Hepburn, Jon Bon Jovi, Celine Dion, Mariah Carey, and Jack Nicklaus's golf brand, Golden Bear.

In 2014, Ted joined DHX Media as senior vice president of licensing in Hollywood, and for over three years, he oversaw the rollout of entertainment brands such as the Teletubbies, Inspector Gadget, Felix the Cat, Space Invaders, and Mega Man.

His book, *Get To Be Happy*, a powerful reframe of how we look at life, has won numerous awards, including being a finalist for the prestigious Eric Hoffer Book Award, and is an IndieBRAG Honoree. Ted lives with his wife and two children in Orlando, Florida. You can find out more about Ted and the Get To Principle at tedlarkins.com or by emailing ted@tedlarkins.com.

NEW! Only from Simple Truths®

IGNITE READS
spark impact in just one hour

IGNITE READS IS A NEW SERIES OF 1-HOUR READS WRITTEN BY WORLD-RENOWNED EXPERTS!

These captivating books will help you become the best version of yourself, allowing for new opportunities in your personal and professional life. Accelerate your career and expand your knowledge with these powerful books written on today's hottest ideas.

TRENDING BUSINESS AND PERSONAL GROWTH TOPICS

 Read in an hour or less

 Leading experts and authors

 Bold design and captivating content

EXCLUSIVELY AVAILABLE ON SIMPLETRUTHS.COM

Need a training framework?
Engage your team with discussion guides and PowerPoints for training events or meetings.

Want your own branded editions?
Express gratitude, appreciation, and instill positive perceptions to staff or clients by adding your organization's logo to your edition of the book.

Add a supplemental visual experience
to any meeting, training, or event.

Contact us for special corporate discounts!
(800) 900-3427 x247 or simpletruths@sourcebooks.com

LOVED WHAT YOU READ AND WANT MORE?

Sign up today and be the FIRST to receive advance copies of Simple Truths® NEW releases written and signed by expert authors. Enjoy a complete package of supplemental materials that can help you host or lead a successful event. This high-value program will uplift you to be the best version of yourself!

— SIMPLE TRUTHS —
ELITE CLUB
ONE MONTH. ONE BOOK. ONE HOUR.

Your monthly dose of motivation, inspiration, and personal growth.